MW00442548

EASY PAELLA COOKBOOK

50 DELICIOUS ONE POT MEALS

By
BookSumo Press
Copyright © by Saxonberg Associates

Published by
BookSumo Press, a DBA of Saxonberg Associates
http://www.booksumo.com/

ABOUT THE AUTHOR.

BookSumo Press is a publisher of unique, easy, and healthy cookbooks.

Our cookbooks span all topics and all subjects. If you want a deep dive into the possibilities of cooking with any type of ingredient. Then BookSumo Press is your go to place for robust yet simple and delicious cookbooks and recipes. Whether you are looking for great tasting pressure cooker recipes or authentic ethic and cultural food. BookSumo Press has a delicious and easy cookbook for you.

With simple ingredients, and even simpler step-by-step instructions BookSumo cookbooks get everyone in the kitchen chefing delicious meals.

BookSumo is an independent publisher of books operating in the beautiful Garden State (NJ) and our team of chefs and kitchen experts are here to teach, eat, and be merry!

INTRODUCTION

Welcome to *The Effortless Chef Series*! Thank you for taking the time to purchase this cookbook.

Come take a journey into the delights of easy cooking. The point of this cookbook and all BookSumo Press cookbooks is to exemplify the effortless nature of cooking simply.

In this book we focus on cooking Paellas. You will find that even though the recipes are simple, the taste of the dishes are quite amazing.

So will you take an adventure in simple cooking? If the answer is yes please consult the table of contents to find the dishes you are most interested in.

Once you are ready, jump right in and start cooking.

— BookSumo Press

TABLE OF CONTENTS

ANY ISSUES? CONTACT US

If you find that something important to you is missing from this book please contact us at info@booksumo.com.

We will take your concerns into consideration when the 2nd edition of this book is published. And we will keep you updated!

— BookSumo Press

LEGAL NOTES

COMMON ABBREVIATIONS

cup(s)	C.
tablespoon	tbsp
teaspoon	tsp
ounce	oz.
pound	lb

*All units used are standard American measurements

Chapter 1: Easy Paella Recipes

No-Meat Paella

Ingredients

- 1 pinch saffron
- 1 medium eggplant, cut into large chunks
- 3 tbsp olive oil
- 1 onion, chopped
- 2 garlic cloves, crushed
- 1 yellow pepper, finely chopped
- 1 red bell pepper, finely chopped
- 2 tsp paprika
- 225 g arborio rice
- 2 1/2 C. vegetable broth
- 1 (19 oz.) can diced tomatoes
- salt and pepper
- 1 C. mushroom, sliced
- 1 C. green beans, cut into segments
- 1 (19 oz.) can chickpeas, rinsed and drained

Directions

- In a small bowl, place the saffron and pour 3 tbsp of water and keep aside.
- In a colander, place the eggplant chunks and sprinkle with the salt and keep aside for about 30 minutes.
- Rinse and drain well.
- In a skillet, heat the oil and sauté the eggplant, peppers, garlic and onion for about 5 minutes.

- Stir in the paprika and rice and then add the tomatoes, broth, saffron, salt and black pepper.
- Bring to a boil and simmer, stirring occasionally for about 15 minutes.
- Gently, fold in the chickpeas, green beans and mushrooms and simmer for about 15 minutes.
- Serve immediately.

Amount per serving: 6

Timing Information:

Preparation	30 mins
Total Time	1 hr 30 mins

Nutritional Information:

Calories	372.1
Cholesterol	0.0mg
Sodium	279.7mg
Carbohydrates	65.8g
Protein	10.1g

* Percent Daily Values are based on a 2,000 calorie diet.

PAELLA IN TRADITIONAL SPANISH STYLE

Ingredients

- 3 C. calasparra rice
- 8 C. hot chicken stock
- 1 large onion, diced
- 3 garlic cloves, minced
- 1 large bell pepper, diced
- 10 -15 flat green beans
- 4 plum tomatoes, diced
- 0.5 (4 oz.) can tomato paste
- 15 large shrimp, peeled and deveined
- 2 -3 lb. rabbit
- 4 links chorizo sausages, sliced into 1 inch pieces
- 1/2 C. fresh parsley
- 2 -3 tbsp fresh thyme
- 1/2 tbsp paprika
- 1 pinch saffron
- 3 lemons, quartered

Directions

- Separate the rabbit legs and cut the remaining meat into small slices.
- In 2 different bowls, place the rabbit meat and shrimp and sprinkle with the salt.
- Grease a paella pan with olive oil on high heat and cook the chorizo for about 1-2 minutes.
- Transfer the chorizo to a plate.
- In the same pan, cook the rabbit for about 2-3 minutes and transfer the rabbit to a plate.
- In the same pan, sauté the bell pepper, onion and garlic till softened.

- Stir in the tomatoes and cook for some time.
- Push the onion mixture to one side of the pan and add the tomato paste and cook for about 1-2 minutes.
- Add the chorizo, rabbit, herbs and paprika and stir to combine with the onion mixture.
- Stir in the rice and cook for about 1-1 1/2 minutes and stir in the saffron.
- Add enough broth to cover the rice mixture and bring to a boil.
- Reduce the heat to medium and cook for about 5-10 minutes, adding the required broth and stirring occasionally.
- Cook for about 10-20 minutes, adding broth as required.
- In the last 8 minutes of cooking, place the shrimp on top and cook, turning once after 2-4 minutes.
- Remove everything from the heat and keep aside covered for about 10-20 minutes before serving.
- Serve hot with a garnishing of lemon wedges.

Amount per serving: 6

Timing Information:

Preparation	40 mins
Total Time	1 hr

Nutritional Information:

Calories	912.9
Cholesterol	149.8mg
Sodium	1183.2mg
Carbohydrates	101.2g
Protein	58.6g

* Percent Daily Values are based on a 2,000 calorie diet.

HEALTHY VEGETABLES PAELLA

Ingredients

- 2 tbsp olive oil
- 1 1/2 C. chopped onions
- 1 red pepper, chopped
- 2 tsp chopped garlic
- 1 C. instant brown rice
- 1 (15 oz.) cans stewed tomatoes
- 1 (15 oz.) cans vegetable broth
- 1 tsp crushed red pepper flakes

- 2 C. zucchini, cut in 1-inch cubes
- 1 (6 1/2 oz.) jars artichoke hearts, drained
- 1 C. carrot, chopped
- 1/2 C. frozen peas, thawed
- 1/4 C. fresh parsley, chopped

Directions

- In a large pan, heat the oil on high heat and sauté the red pepper, onion and garlic for about 5 minutes.
- Stir in the rice and add the broth, tomatoes and red pepper flakes and bring to a boil.
- Reduce the heat to medium-low and simmer, covered for about 10 minutes, stirring occasionally.
- Stir in the artichoke, zucchini and carrots and simmer, covered for about 15-20 minutes.
- Stir in the peas and parsley and simmer for a few more minutes.

Amount per serving: 8

Timing Information:

Preparation	30 mins
Total Time	1 hr 30 mins

Nutritional Information:

Calories	139.0
Cholesterol	0.0mg
Sodium	167.4mg
Carbohydrates	23.8g
Protein	3.6g

* Percent Daily Values are based on a 2,000 calorie diet.

PAELLA IN PORTUGUESE STYLE

Ingredients

- 1 chicken, cut into pieces
- 1 small onion, chopped
- 2 ham hocks, optional
- salt and pepper
- 1/4 C. extra virgin olive oil
- 2 garlic cloves
- 2 C. rice
- 1/2 lb raw peeled shrimp
- 1/2 lb clam

- 1/2 lb mussels
- 1/2 lb sea scallops
- 3/4 lb chorizo sausage
- 1 red bell pepper
- 1 C. chicken broth
- 3/4 C. white wine
- 1/4 tsp saffron
- 1/2 C. frozen peas

Directions

- Sprinkle the chicken with the salt and black pepper.
- In a large pan, heat the oil and sauté the ham hock and chicken till golden brown.
- Transfer the chicken pieces to a plate.
- Add the rice, onion and garlic and sauté for a few minutes.
- Place the chicken, seafood and sausage over the rice mixture.
- Add the broth, wine, bell pepper and saffron and simmer, covered for about 20 minutes.
- Stir in the peas and simmer, covered for about 10 minutes.

Amount per serving: 2

Timing Information:

Preparation	15 mins
Total Time	1 hr 3 mins

Nutritional Information:

Calories	2542.5
Cholesterol	680.7mg
Sodium	3102.8mg
Carbohydrates	191.8g
Protein	175.9g

* Percent Daily Values are based on a 2,000 calorie diet.

CLASSICAL ONE-POT HOT POT

Ingredients

- 1 tbsp olive oil
- 1/2 lb chunk chicken
- 1 C. rice, uncooked
- 1 medium chopped onion
- 2 tsp garlic, minced
- 1 1/2 C. chicken broth
- 1 (8 oz.) cans stewed tomatoes, chopped reserving liquid
- 1/2-1 tsp paprika
- 1/8-1/4 tsp ground red pepper
- 1/8-1/4 tsp saffron
- 1/2 lb medium shrimp, peeled and deveined
- 1 small red pepper, cut into strips
- 1 small green pepper, cut into strips
- 1/2 C. frozen green pea

Directions

- In a Dutch oven, heat the oil and stir fry the chicken till golden brown.
- Stir in the rice, onion and garlic and cook, stirring occasionally till the rice becomes golden brown.
- Add the broth, tomatoes with liquid, saffron, paprika and red pepper and bring to a boil.
- Reduce the heat and simmer, covered for about 10 minutes.

Amount per serving: 6

Timing Information:

Preparation	20 mins
Total Time	55 mins

Nutritional Information:

Calories	284.3
Cholesterol	81.0mg
Sodium	542.4mg
Carbohydrates	34.1g
Protein	20.7g

* Percent Daily Values are based on a 2,000 calorie diet.

Stunning Paella

Ingredients

- 1 lb fresh shrimp
- 1 lb squid
- 1 lb mussels
- 2 C. short-grain rice
- 1 onion, minced
- 1 tbsp tomato paste
- 1/2 green pepper

- 1/2 red pepper
- 2 garlic cloves, minced
- 3 tbsp olive oil
- 1/2 tsp saffron thread
- salt
- pepper
- 5 C. water

Directions

- In a large pan, heat half of the oil and sauté the onion for about 3 minutes.
- Stir in the bell peppers and tomato paste and sauté for about 2-3 minutes.
- Stir in rice, squids, saffron, salt and black pepper and sauté for about 2-3 minutes.
- Add the warm water and the remaining oil and cook till the liquid is absorbed.
- Add the mussels and shrimp and cook, stirring occasionally for about 10 minutes.

Amount per serving: 5

Timing Information:

Preparation	5 mins
Total Time	30 mins

Nutritional Information:

Calories	603.9
Cholesterol	351.8mg
Sodium	850.3mg
Carbohydrates	74.6g
Protein	43.2g

* Percent Daily Values are based on a 2,000 calorie diet.

Paella in Mediterranean Style

Ingredients

- 3 tbsp olive oil
- 1 medium onion, chopped
- 2 tbsp fresh minced garlic
- 1 tsp dried chili pepper flakes
- 1 small red bell pepper, seeded and chopped
- 1 C. frozen artichoke heart, thawed
- 3/4 C. sliced pitted olive
- 1 (14 oz.) cans chicken broth
- 1 C. water
- 1 C. uncooked long-grain white rice
- salt, to taste
- 1/2 tsp paprika
- 1 pinch saffron thread
- black pepper
- 2 C. cooked chicken, chopped
- 3/4 C. frozen green pea, thawed

Directions

- In a large skillet, heat the oil on medium heat and sauté the onion, bell pepper, garlic and chili flakes for about 3 minutes.
- Stir in the olives and artichokes and sauté for about 2 minutes.
- Add the water and broth and bring to a boil.
- Reduce the heat to medium-low and simmer, covered for about 15 minutes.
- Stir in the chicken and peas and simmer, covered for about 5-7 minutes.
- Remove everything from the heat and keep aside, covered for about 5 minutes before serving.

Amount per serving: 4

Timing Information:

| Preparation | 20 mins |
| Total Time | 45 mins |

Nutritional Information:

Calories	484.3
Cholesterol	52.5mg
Sodium	1207.2mg
Carbohydrates	51.1g
Protein	26.6g

* Percent Daily Values are based on a 2,000 calorie diet.

CLASSICO PAELLA

Ingredients

- 2 tbsp olive oil, divided.
- 2 1/2-3 lb. chicken, cut into 8 pieces
- 8 oz. chorizo sausages, cut into 1 inch pieces
- 2 cloves garlic, chopped
- 1 medium yellow onion, chopped
- 1 C. uncooked white rice
- 1 tsp saffron
- 2 C. beef broth
- 1 large roasted red pepper, cut into thin strips
- 1/4 C. chopped green onion
- 1/4 C. chopped fresh cilantro
- 1 jalapeno pepper, seeded and chopped
- 1/4 tsp crushed red pepper flakes
- 1/2 lb medium shrimp, shelled and deveined
- 1/2 C. green peas

Directions

- In a paella pan, heat 1 tbsp of the oil and stir fry the chicken and sausage for about 20 minutes.
- Transfer the chicken and sausage to a paper towel lined plate and cover with a foil paper to keep warm.
- Drain off the fat from the pan and wipe it with some paper towel.
- In the same pan, heat the remaining oil and sauté the onion and garlic for about 5 minutes.

- Stir in the rice and saffron and stir fry for about 2 minutes.
- Add the broth and bring to a boil.
- Reduce the heat to low and simmer, covered for about 30 minutes.
- Stir in the cooked chicken, sausage and remaining ingredients except the shrimp and peas and simmer, stirring occasionally for about 15 minutes.
- Stir in the shrimp and peas and simmer for about 5 minutes.

Amount per serving: 6

Timing Information:

Preparation	30 mins
Total Time	1 hr 30 mins

Nutritional Information:

Calories	787.1
Cholesterol	222.8mg
Sodium	1117.0mg
Carbohydrates	30.8g
Protein	53.5g

* Percent Daily Values are based on a 2,000 calorie diet.

Summer Veggie Paella

Ingredients

- 2 tbsp olive oil
- 1 C. chopped onion
- 1 C. chopped red pepper
- 2 tsp finely chopped fresh garlic
- 1 C. uncooked long grain rice
- 1 (14 1/2 oz.) can stewed tomatoes
- 1 (14 1/2 oz.) can vegetable broth
- 1 C. finely chopped carrot
- 1 tsp paprika
- 1 (6 1/2 oz.) jar marinated artichoke hearts, drained
- 1 C. eggplant, cubed
- 1 C. zucchini, cubed
- 1/2 C. frozen peas, thawed
- 1/4 C. chopped fresh parsley

Directions

- In a large pan, heat the oil on medium-high heat and sauté the red pepper, onion and garlic for about 2-3 minutes.
- Stir in the rice and stir fry for about 1 minute.
- Add the broth, tomatoes, carrots and paprika and bring to a boil.
- Reduce the heat to medium-low and simmer, covered for about 10 minutes, stirring once half way.
- Stir in the eggplant, artichokes and zucchini simmer, stirring occasionally for about 10-12 minutes.
- Stir in the peas and parsley and simmer for about 3-4 minutes.

Amount per serving: 8

Timing Information:

| Preparation | 35 mins |
| Total Time | 1 hr 5 mins |

Nutritional Information:

Calories	173.5
Cholesterol	0.0mg
Sodium	169.4mg
Carbohydrates	31.8g
Protein	4.3g

* Percent Daily Values are based on a 2,000 calorie diet.

PAELLA FOREVER

Ingredients

- 1 tbsp olive oil
- 3/4 lb large shrimp, peeled and deveined
- 3/4 tsp salt, divided
- 1/4 tsp ground black pepper, divided
- 1/2 C. chorizo sausage, thinly sliced
- 2 boneless skinless chicken thighs, quartered
- 1 C. onion, chopped
- 3 garlic cloves, minced
- 1/2 C. tomatoes, chopped
- 1 tbsp capers, drained
- 1/4 tsp saffron thread, crushed
- 1 C. Arborio rice
- 2/3 C. white wine
- 14 oz. fat-free low-chicken broth
- 1/2 C. frozen green pea
- 1/4 C. water
- 18 mussels
- 2 1/2 tbsp roasted red peppers, chopped
- 2 tbsp cilantro, chopped

Directions

- In a large pan, heat the oil on medium-high and add the shrimp, salt and black pepper.
- Stir fry the shrimp for about 4 minutes and transfer it into a bowl.
- Add the chorizo and cook for about 1 minute and transfer into a bowl.
- Add the chicken, salt and black pepper and sear for about 2 minutes per side.
- Add the onion and garlic and stir fry for about 2 minutes.

- Stir in the tomato, capers and saffron and stir fry for about 1 minute.
- Add the rice, broth, wine, salt and black pepper and bring to a boil.
- Reduce the heat and simmer, covered for about 25 minutes.
- Stir in the shrimp, chorizo, mussels, peas and water and simmer for about 8 minutes.
- Stir in the bell peppers and cilantro and remove from the heat.
- Keep aside, covered for about 3 minutes before serving.

Amount per serving: 6

Timing Information:

Preparation	20 mins
Total Time	50 mins

Nutritional Information:

Calories	398.2
Cholesterol	120.8mg
Sodium	1142.9mg
Carbohydrates	36.8g
Protein	27.7g

* Percent Daily Values are based on a 2,000 calorie diet.

GRAND THEFT PAELLA

Ingredients

- 3 1/4 C. vegetable broth
- 1 1/2 tbsp chopped parsley
- 1 tsp dried basil
- 1/2 tsp saffron
- 1/4 tsp ground cumin
- 6 tbsp olive oil
- 4 tbsp pine nuts
- 1 large onion, chopped fine
- 8 garlic cloves, minced

- 1 medium green bell pepper, chopped fine
- 3/4 C. pimento stuffed olive, chopped
- 5 C. spinach leaves, destemmed and chopped
- 1 1/2 C. rice
- 1/2 C. parmesan cheese, grated

Directions

- In a pan, mix together the broth, herbs, saffron and cumin on low heat
- In a large paella pan, heat the oil and stir fry the pine nuts till lightly toasted.
- Add the bell pepper, onion and garlic till tender.
- Add the spinach and olives and cook till the spinach is wilted.
- Sir in the rice and add the broth mixture and bring to a boil.
- Reduce the heat and simmer, covered for about 25 minutes.
- Stir in the cheese and remove from the heat.

Amount per serving: 6

Timing Information:

Preparation	15 mins
Total Time	55 mins

Nutritional Information:

Calories	440.3
Cholesterol	8.6mg
Sodium	589.4mg
Carbohydrates	52.7g
Protein	10.2g

* Percent Daily Values are based on a 2,000 calorie diet.

Restaurant Style Paella

Ingredients

- 2 tsp sesame oil
- 125 g shallots
- 20 g gingerroot
- 2 garlic cloves
- 400 g chicken breasts
- salt and pepper
- 250 g orzo pasta

- 1 1/2 tsp smoked paprika
- 600 ml chicken stock
- 225 -250 g prawns
- 1/4 C. lemon juice
- 3 tsp soy sauce
- 1/3 C. coriander leaves

Directions

- In a large pan, heat the oil on medium heat and sauté the shallots, garlic and ginger till tender.
- Add the chicken, salt and black pepper and cook till golden brown.
- Stir in the orzo and paprika and cook till it just starts to absorb the flavors.
- Add enough broth to cover the mixture and bring to a boil.
- Simmer, stirring occasionally for about 15 minutes.
- Stir in the prawns, soy sauce, lemon juice and seasoning and cook till done.
- Remove everything from the heat and keep aside, covered for about 3-5 minutes before serving.
- Stir in the coriander and serve.

Amount per serving: 4

Timing Information:

Preparation	20 mins
Total Time	50 mins

Nutritional Information:

Calories	555.9
Cholesterol	139.4mg
Sodium	860.0mg
Carbohydrates	61.0g
Protein	42.1g

* Percent Daily Values are based on a 2,000 calorie diet.

SWEDISH PAELLA

Ingredients

- 2 tbsp onions, minced
- 1 tbsp butter
- 1 C. rice
- 2 C. water
- 2 tsp salt
- 1/2 tsp garlic powder
- 1/2 tsp black pepper
- 1 pinch saffron threads

- 1/4 red pepper, cut into strips
- 1/4 green pepper, cut into strips
- 1/4-1/2 lb shrimp, cleaned
- 1 lb chicken, cut into small pieces
- 1/2 C. frozen peas
- black olives, sliced (to garnish)

Directions

- Set your oven to 350 degrees F before doing anything else.
- For the pilaf, in a large pan, melt the butter and stir fry the rice and onion till golden brown.
- Add the water and salt and bring to a boil.
- Reduce the heat to low and simmer, covered for about 20 minutes.
- For the paella, in a baking dish, mix together the cooked pilaf, chicken, bell peppers and spices and cook everything in the oven for 10-20 minutes.
- Stir in the peas and shrimp and cook for about 5 minutes more.
- Serve with a garnishing of olives.

Amount per serving: 4

Timing Information:

Preparation	30 mins
Total Time	1 hr 15 mins

Nutritional Information:

Calories	485.6
Cholesterol	128.4mg
Sodium	1451.0mg
Carbohydrates	42.9g
Protein	29.3g

* Percent Daily Values are based on a 2,000 calorie diet.

MOUNTAIN-STYLE PAELLA

Ingredients

- 2 (14 oz.) cans chicken broth
- 3/4 C. white wine
- 1/4 C. vermouth, optional
- 1 tsp turmeric
- 2 tsp paprika
- 1 lb boneless skinless chicken thighs, cut into strips
- 1/2 lb Italian sausage, casing removed and cut into small pieces
- 1 tbsp olive oil
- 1 large green bell pepper, cut into thin slices
- 1 large red bell pepper, cut into thin slices

- 1 large white onion, halved and sliced thin
- 2 jalapeno peppers, seeded and chopped
- 5 cloves garlic, minced
- 1 tsp thyme
- 1 tsp oregano
- 1/2 tsp ground coriander
- 2 C. rice (short grain works best)
- 1 lb medium shrimp, raw, shells and tails removed
- 4 roma tomatoes, chopped
- 1 1/2 C. fresh green beans, sliced into ½ inch pieces
- 1/2 C. black olives, sliced

Directions

- In a pan, mix together the broth, vermouth, wine, paprika and turmeric and bring to a gentle simmer, stirring occasionally.

- In a large skillet, brown the sausage completely and transfer onto a plate.
- In the same skillet, brown the chicken strips completely and transfer onto a plate.
- In the same skillet, heat the oil and sauté the peppers, onion and garlic till tender.
- Add the spices in the hot broth mixture and stir to combine.
- In the same skillet, add the broth mixture, chicken and sausage and bring to a boil.
- Add the rice and gently stir to combine and tuck the shrimp in the rice mixture.
- Place the tomatoes, beans and olives on top.
- Bring to a boil and reduce the heat.
- Cook, covered for about 20 minutes.
- Remove everything from the heat and keep aside, covered for about 10 minutes before serving.

Amount per serving: 8

Timing Information:

Preparation	30 mins
Total Time	1 hr 10 mins

Nutritional Information:

Calories	477.1
Cholesterol	135.0mg
Sodium	1109.0mg
Carbohydrates	49.8g
Protein	31.2g

* Percent Daily Values are based on a 2,000 calorie diet.

PAELLA FOR CELEBRATIONS

Ingredients

- 6 boneless skinless chicken breasts
- 3 chorizo sausage, sliced
- 18 large shrimp, shelled & deveined
- 1 lb mussels
- 2 tbsp olive oil
- 5 C. chicken broth

- 1 C. white wine
- 1 pinch saffron
- 1 onion, chopped
- 3 garlic cloves, chopped
- salt, pepper, paprika
- 1 C. peas
- 1 (4 oz.) jars pimientos
- 3 C. arborio rice

Directions

- Set your oven to 400 degrees F before doing anything else.
- In a skillet, heat 1 tbsp of the oil and brown the sausage completely and transfer into a plate.
- In the same skillet, heat more oil and brown the chicken completely and transfer onto a plate.
- In the same skillet, heat the remaining oil and sauté the onion and garlic till softened.
- Add the wine, broth and spices and bring to a boil, stirring continuously.
- Cook till the liquid reduces slightly.

- Stir in the sausage, chicken, pimentos and peas and cook in the oven for about 10 minutes.
- Serve with a garnishing of parsley.

Amount per serving: 8

Timing Information:

Preparation	30 mins
Total Time	1 hr 30 mins

Nutritional Information:

Calories	639.6
Cholesterol	110.9mg
Sodium	1003.8mg
Carbohydrates	68.9g
Protein	45.1g

* Percent Daily Values are based on a 2,000 calorie diet.

RICH PAELLA

Ingredients

- 2 C. quinoa, rinsed well
- 2 tbsp olive oil
- 1 lb chorizo sausage, peeled
- 5 garlic cloves, coarsely chopped
- 2 red bell peppers, seeded and roughly chopped
- 1 serrano pepper, minced
- 1 onion, chopped
- 2 tsp salt
- 1/2 tsp black pepper
- 1 C. frozen lima beans
- 1 (15 oz.) cans cannellini beans
- 2 tomatoes, seeded and chopped
- 4 C. chicken stock
- 2 tbsp parsley, chopped
- 2 lemons, cut into wedges

Directions

- In a bowl, soak the quinoa in cold water for about 15 minutes and drain well.
- Heat a large pan on medium-high heat and cook the quinoa for about 15 minutes, stirring occasionally.
- Transfer the quinoa into a bowl.
- In the same pan, heat the oil and cook the sausage for about 10 minutes, breaking the sausage into little pieces.
- Stir in the bell peppers, onion, serrano, salt and black pepper and sauté for about 5 minutes.
- Stir in the tomatoes, both beans and broth and bring to a boil.

- Reduce the heat to low and simmer for about 15 minutes.
- Remove everything from the heat and keep aside, covered for about 10 minutes before serving.
- Serve hot with a garnishing of parsley.

Amount per serving: 8

Timing Information:

Preparation	15 mins
Total Time	1 hr 15 mins

Nutritional Information:

Calories	582.6
Cholesterol	53.5mg
Sodium	1633.1mg
Carbohydrates	50.8g
Protein	27.8g

* Percent Daily Values are based on a 2,000 calorie diet.

Authentic Seafood Paella in Spanish Style

Ingredients

- 2 1/2 lb. chicken parts
- 1/4 C. olive oil
- 1 medium onion, finely diced
- 4 garlic cloves, minced
- 2 tsp salt
- fresh ground pepper
- 1/2 tsp paprika
- 1 large red bell pepper, roasted, peeled, seeded, and diced
- 1/2 C. sliced green onion
- 1 lb squid, cleaned, sacs cut into rings
- 1/2 tsp saffron thread
- 1 lb large raw shrimp, peeled and deveined
- 3 C. short-grain rice
- 6 C. warm chicken stock
- 1 1/2 lb. small live clams
- 1 C. frozen peas

Directions

- Cut each leg of the chicken into 4 pieces and each breast half into 3 pieces.
- In a paella pan, heat the oil on low heat and sauté the onion and garlic till the onion just starts to sizzle.
- Increase the heat to medium and cook the chicken pieces with the paprika, salt and black pepper in batches till golden brown.
- Add the squid, peppers, green onion, salt, black pepper and crumbled saffron.
- Stir in the rice and stir fry for about 1 minute.

- Add enough warm broth to cover the mixture and top it with the shrimp and clams.
- Simmer for about 10 minutes.
- Top everything with the peas and simmer for about 10 minutes more.

Amount per serving: 8

Timing Information:

Preparation	1 hr
Total Time	1 hr 45 mins

Nutritional Information:

Calories	887.3
Cholesterol	344.9mg
Sodium	1820.9mg
Carbohydrates	76.8g
Protein	74.1g

* Percent Daily Values are based on a 2,000 calorie diet.

MIDWEEK PAELLA

Ingredients

- 1/2 lb hot Italian sausage, cut into 1/2 inch cubes
- 1 onion, chopped
- 1 green bell pepper, chopped
- 2 garlic cloves, minced
- 1 C. long-grain rice
- 14 oz. canned tomatoes, chopped
- 1 C. chicken stock
- 1/2 tsp ground turmeric
- 1/4 tsp cayenne pepper
- 1 lb boneless skinless chicken breast, remove all visible fat and cut into 1 inch cubes
- salt and pepper
- 1 green onion, chopped diagonally

Directions

- In a large microwave safe dish, mix together the sausage, green pepper, onion and garlic.
- Microwave on high for about 4-6 minutes, stirring once half way.
- Add the rice, tomatoes, cayenne pepper, turmeric and broth and stir to combine.

- Cover the dish and microwave it on high for about 8-10 minutes.
- Stir everything well, cover the dish and microwave on medium for about 7-9 minutes.
- Remove everything from the heat and keep it aside, covered for about 5 minutes before serving.
- Serve hot with a garnishing of green onions.

Amount per serving: 4

Timing Information:

Preparation	15 mins
Total Time	45 mins

Nutritional Information:

Calories	549.8
Cholesterol	110.5mg
Sodium	704.6mg
Carbohydrates	48.5g
Protein	40.5g

* Percent Daily Values are based on a 2,000 calorie diet.

Distinctive Paella

Ingredients

- 2 tbsp vegetable oil
- 1 onion, sliced
- 1 red pepper, cored, seeded and sliced
- 1 garlic clove, crushed
- 200 g long grain rice
- 180 g smoked ham, roughly diced
- 900 ml chicken stock
- 1/2 tsp paprika
- 1/2 tsp turmeric
- 100 g large shrimp
- 100 g frozen peas
- salt & freshly ground black pepper

Directions

- In a large pan, heat the oil and sauté the onion for about 3-4 minutes.
- Add the rice and garlic and stir fry for about 1 minute.
- Stir in the remaining ingredients except the prawns and peas and bring to a boil.
- Simmer for about 12 minutes.
- Stir in the prawns and peas and simmer for about 3-4 minutes.
- Serve immediately.

Amount per serving: 4

Timing Information:

Preparation	20 mins
Total Time	45 mins

Nutritional Information:

Calories	484.0
Cholesterol	75.6mg
Sodium	1169.7mg
Carbohydrates	57.4g
Protein	26.7g

* Percent Daily Values are based on a 2,000 calorie diet.

Mexican Paella

Ingredients

- 3 tbsp olive oil
- 1 large onion, diced
- 6 garlic cloves, minced
- 1/2 tsp red chili pepper flakes
- 2 tsp salt
- 1 tbsp chili powder
- 1 tbsp sweet paprika
- 2 tsp oregano
- 1 large red pepper, chopped
- 1 large yellow pepper, chopped
- 4 medium tomatoes, ripe, chopped
- 1 1/4 C. arborio rice
- 3 C. hot vegetable stock
- 1/2 lb green beans, trimmed and sliced into 1 inch lengths
- fresh ground pepper
- 1/2 bunch cilantro, chopped
- 1/2 bunch parsley, chopped
- 1 bunch scallion, minced
- aged cheddar cheese or parmesan cheese

Directions

- In a large pan, heat the oil and sauté the onion till tender.
- Add the garlic, chili flakes and salt and sauté for a few minutes.
- Stir in the tomatoes, peppers, herbs, spices and salt and simmer, covered for about 10 minutes.
- Stir in the rice till it is coated with the mixture.
- Add the hot broth and bring to a boil.

- Reduce the heat to low and simmer, covered for about 30 minutes.
- Meanwhile steam the green beans till the desired doneness.
- Add the green beans, herbs and black pepper in the pan and stir to combine.
- Serve with a garnishing of cheese and scallions.

Amount per serving: 4

Timing Information:

Preparation	10 mins
Total Time	55 mins

Nutritional Information:

Calories	412.4
Cholesterol	0.0mg
Sodium	1202.0mg
Carbohydrates	71.5g
Protein	8.3g

* Percent Daily Values are based on a 2,000 calorie diet.

INCREDIBLY DELICIOUS PAELLA

Ingredients

- 1 lb extra-large shrimp, peeled and deveined
- salt and pepper
- olive oil
- 2 tbsp garlic, minced
- 1 lb boneless skinless chicken thighs, trimmed of excess fat and halved crosswise
- 1 red bell pepper, seeded and cut pole to pole into 1/2-inch-wide strips
- 8 oz. chorizo sausage, Spanish sliced 1/2 inch thick on the bias
- 1 medium onion, chopped fine
- 1 (14 1/2 oz.) cans diced tomatoes, drained, minced, and drained again
- 2 C. arborio rice
- 3 C. low chicken broth
- 2/3 C. dry white wine
- 1/2 tsp saffron thread, crumbled
- 1 bay leaf
- 1/8 tsp dried thyme
- paprika, as required
- 1 tsp ground cumin
- 1 dozen mussels, scrubbed and debearded
- 1/2 C. frozen green pea, thawed
- 2 tsp fresh parsley leaves, chopped
- 1 lemon, cut into wedges, for serving

Directions

- Set your oven to 350 degrees F before doing anything else and arrange the oven rack to the lower-middle position.

- In a bowl, add the shrimp, 1 tsp of the garlic, 1 tbsp of the oil, salt and black pepper and toss to coat well.
- Refrigerate, covered till serving.
- In another bowl, add the chicken and season with the salt and black pepper.
- In a large Dutch oven, heat 2 tsp of the oil on medium-high heat and sauté the peppers for about 3-4 minutes.
- Transfer the peppers onto a plate.
- In the same pan, heat 1 tsp of the oil and cook the chicken for about 3 minutes per side.
- Transfer the chicken into another plate.
- Reduce the heat to medium and cook the chorizo for about 4-5 minutes.
- Transfer the chorizo to the plate with the chicken.
- In the same Dutch oven, heat 2 tbsp of the oil on medium heat and sauté the onion for about 3 minutes.
- Add the remaining garlic and sauté for about 1 minute.
- Add the tomatoes and cook for about 3 minutes.
- Add the rice and stir fry for about 1-2 minutes.
- Add the wine, broth, saffron, paprika, cumin, thyme, bay leaf and salt and bring to a boil on medium-high heat.
- Cover and cook in the oven for about 30 minutes.
- Stir in the chicken and chorizo, cover, and cook everything in the oven for about 15 minutes.
- Insert the mussels into rice mixture, hinged side down and place the shrimp over the rice.
- Top everything with the peppers, cover, and cook it in the oven for about 10-12 minutes.

- Remove everything from the oven and keep it aside, covered, for about 5 minutes before serving.
- Serve hot with a garnishing of parsley and lemon wedges.

Amount per serving: 6

Timing Information:

Preparation	45 mins
Total Time	46 mins

Nutritional Information:

Calories	668.6
Cholesterol	200.4mg
Sodium	1120.0mg
Carbohydrates	66.7g
Protein	47.3g

* Percent Daily Values are based on a 2,000 calorie diet.

GOURMET DINNER PAELLA

Ingredients

- 1 lb chorizo sausage, removed from casings
- 1/2 C. onion, diced
- 2 garlic cloves, finely chopped
- 1 C. pumpkin, cooked
- 1/2 C. frozen peas
- 1/2 tsp cinnamon
- 1/2 tsp ground nutmeg
- 1/8 tsp ground cloves
- fresh parsley
- fresh snipped chives
- Roasted Tomatoes
- 2 medium tomatoes, chopped
- 1 tbsp honey
- drizzle olive oil
- salt and pepper
- Saffron Rice
- 4 C. chicken broth
- 1 pinch saffron thread
- 1 C. arborio rice

Directions

- Set your oven to 325 degrees F before doing anything else and lightly grease a baking sheet.
- For the roasted tomatoes, in a bowl, add the tomatoes, oil, honey, salt and black pepper and toss to coat.
- Transfer the tomato mixture onto the prepared baking sheet and cook in the oven for about 20 minutes.
- For the rice, in a pan, add the broth and bring to a boil.
- Stir in the rice and saffron and bring to a boil.

- Reduce the heat to low and simmer, covered for about 20 minutes.
- For the paella, heat a large skillet on medium heat and stir fry the sausage, onion and garlic breaking the sausage into pieces.
- Stir in the cooked rice, pumpkin, roasted tomatoes, peas and spices and simmer, covered for about 5-10 minutes.
- Serve hot with a garnishing of chives and parsley.

Amount per serving: 6

Timing Information:

Preparation	20 mins
Total Time	30 mins

Nutritional Information:

Calories	529.9
Cholesterol	66.5mg
Sodium	1459.3mg
Carbohydrates	37.7g
Protein	25.0g

* Percent Daily Values are based on a 2,000 calorie diet.

Island Chicken Paella

Ingredients

- 2 -3 lb. chicken pieces
- 3 tbsp olive oil
- salt and pepper
- 1 medium onion, sliced into thin wedges
- 2 tbsp fresh minced garlic
- 1 C. long-grain white rice, uncooked
- 1 (14 1/2 oz.) can diced tomatoes
- 3 C. chicken broth
- 2 tbsp capers
- 1 tsp cayenne pepper
- 12 Spanish olives, green with pimento, sliced
- 1 C. frozen peas, thawed
- 1 (7 oz.) jar roasted sweet peppers

Directions

- In a large paella pan, heat the oil and cook the chicken with the salt and black pepper till browned from all the sides.
- Transfer the chicken into a bowl.
- In the same pan, sauté the onion and garlic till tender.
- Stir in the rice and stir fry for about 1 minute.
- Stir in the cooked chicken, tomatoes, capers, cayenne pepper and broth and bring to a boil.
- Reduce the heat to very low and simmer, covered for about 30-40 minutes.
- Gently, fold in the peas and olives and top with the pepper strips.

- Simmer, covered for about 3-4 minutes.

Amount per serving: 4

Timing Information:

| Preparation | 25 mins |
| Total Time | 1 hr |

Nutritional Information:

Calories	648.2
Cholesterol	103.5mg
Sodium	829.8mg
Carbohydrates	50.6g
Protein	36.0g

* Percent Daily Values are based on a 2,000 calorie diet.

SOUTH AFRICAN STYLE PAELLA

Ingredients

- 1/4 C. cooking oil
- 3 red sweet peppers, julienned
- 1 large onion, chopped
- 1 lb pork, cubed
- 5 chicken thighs, halved
- 4 C. boiling water
- 1 tsp saffron
- 4 bay leaves
- 2 chicken stock cubes
- 2 lb. kingklip or white perch fillets, cut in strips
- 12 oz. prawns, frozen
- 1 lb rice, uncooked
- salt and pepper
- 8 oz. frozen green peas
- 1 lemon, juice of

Directions

- In a pan, heat the oil and sauté the chicken, pork, onion and pepper till golden brown.
- Reduce the heat to very low and simmer, covered for about 1 hour.
- In a bowl, mix together the boiling water, chicken cubes, saffron and bay leaves.
- Uncover the pan and place the seafood over the meat mixture.
- Top everything with the rice and peas and season the dish with the salt and black pepper.
- Slowly, add the water mixture and cook till all the liquid is absorbed.
- Stir in the lemon juice and serve.

Amount per serving: 6

Timing Information:

Preparation	15 mins
Total Time	2 hrs 15 mins

Nutritional Information:

Calories	951.0
Cholesterol	336.8mg
Sodium	984.6mg
Carbohydrates	80.4g
Protein	81.4g

* Percent Daily Values are based on a 2,000 calorie diet.

PERSIAN PAELLA

Ingredients

- 1 pinch saffron
- 2 tbsp lemon juice
- 2 tbsp olive oil
- 1 tsp agave syrup
- 1 dash sea salt
- 1/2 C. shitake mushrooms
- 1/2 C. water
- 1/4 C. rice wine vinegar
- 2 tbsp soy sauce
- 1 tbsp dulse flakes
- 1 tsp paprika

- Paella Ric
- 1 1/2 C. turnips, chopped
- 1/3 C. pine nuts
- 1/4 C. bell pepper
- 2 tbsp onions
- 1 tsp garlic
- 2 small tomatoes, chopped
- 1/2 C. fresh peas
- 1/4 C. parsley
- 1/4 C. sun-dried tomato, soaked well chopped

Directions

- For the dressing, in a bowl, soak the saffron in lemon juice for about 20 minutes.
- Add the remaining dressing ingredients and stir to combine.
- Meanwhile in a large bowl, mix together all the mushroom marinate ingredients.
- In a food processor, add the bell peppers, turnips, onion, garlic and pine nuts and pulse till a rice like consistency forms.

- Drain the mushrooms from the marinade.
- Transfer the veggie mixture into a bowl with the tomatoes, peas, parsley and dressing and stir to combine.
- Top the salad with the mushrooms and green olives.
- Serve the salad with a sprinkling of paprika.

Amount per serving: 2

Timing Information:

Preparation	20 mins
Total Time	20 mins

Nutritional Information:

Calories	435.3
Cholesterol	28.3mg
Sodium	1260.5mg
Carbohydrates	30.5g
Protein	14.8g

* Percent Daily Values are based on a 2,000 calorie diet.

Americano Paella

Ingredients

- 2 medium ripe tomatoes
- 16 large shrimp, peeled and deveined
- 1 tsp smoked spanish paprika
- fresh ground black pepper
- 1 lb chicken thigh, cut into 1-inch pieces (boneless, skinless)
- 8 oz. Spanish chorizo, cut into 1/4-inch-thick rounds
- 1 -2 tbsp olive oil, as needed
- 1 medium yellow onion, small dice
- 2 medium garlic cloves, finely chopped
- 1 large pinch saffron thread
- kosher salt, to taste
- 4 C. low chicken broth
- 16 mussels
- 2 tbsp coarsely chopped fresh Italian parsley
- 2 medium lemons, cut into 8 wedges each, for serving

Directions

- Set your oven to 350 degrees F before doing anything else and arrange a rack in the middle of the oven.
- Cut the tomatoes in half and remove the seeds.
- Grate the tomato halves in a bowl, leaving the skin. (Pulp and juice should be about 3/4 C.)
- In a bowl, add the shrimp, 1/4 tsp of the paprika, salt and black pepper and toss to coat.

- Refrigerate to marinate before serving.
- In another bowl, add the chicken and sprinkle with the salt and black pepper.
- Heat a paella pan on medium-high heat and cook the sausage for about 2-3 minutes.
- Transfer the sausage in a bowl.
- In the same pan, add the chicken and stir fry for about 6 minutes.
- Transfer the chicken in a bowl.
- Reduce the heat to medium and sauté the onion, salt and black pepper for about 5 minutes.
- Stir in the garlic, saffron and remaining paprika and sauté for about 30 seconds.
- Stir in the tomato pulp with juice and stir fry for about 3 minutes.
- Stir in the rice and increase the heat to medium-high.
- Stir in the broth and place the chicken and chorizo on top.
- Bring to a boil.
- Reduce the heat and simmer, covered for about 10-12 minutes.
- Remove everything from the heat and insert the marinated shrimp and mussels in the rice mixture.
- Cook everything in the oven for about 10-12 minutes.
- Remove the dish from the oven and keep aside, covered for about 5 minutes before serving.
- Serve hot with a garnishing of lemon wedges and parsley.

Amount per serving: 6

Timing Information:

Preparation	15 mins
Total Time	1 hr 45 mins

Nutritional Information:

Calories	592.2
Cholesterol	111.5mg
Sodium	834.8mg
Carbohydrates	61.2g
Protein	33.0g

* Percent Daily Values are based on a 2,000 calorie diet.

ANNABELLE'S PAELLA

Ingredients

- 6 chicken thighs, cut in half
- salt & freshly ground black pepper
- 2 tbsp extra virgin olive oil
- 1/2 tsp saffron threads or 1 tsp turmeric
- 7 C. chicken broth
- 1 (12 oz.) boxes frozen green beans, thawed
- 1 (14 oz.) cans artichoke hearts, drained and chopped into halves
- 2 large onions, minced
- 4 garlic cloves, minced
- 1 tsp red pepper flakes, crushed
- 1 tsp smoked paprika
- 1 (28 oz.) cans Italian plum tomatoes, drained, seeded and chopped
- 3 C. short-grain rice
- 1/2 lb spanish smoked style chorizo sausage, cut into 1/2 inch slices
- 1 red bell pepper, roasted, peeled, seeded and thinly sliced
- 12 medium shrimp, peeled and deveined
- 1 C. frozen peas, thawed
- 12 small fresh clams
- lemon wedge (garnish)

Directions

- Sprinkle the chicken thighs with the salt and black pepper evenly.
- Heat 1 tbsp the oil in each of 2 paella pans.
- Add the chicken in both pans and cook for about 15-20 minutes.

- Transfer the chicken onto a plate.
- Meanwhile in a small pan, toast the saffron threads and with the back of a spoon, crush it in the pan.
- Add 1/2 C. of the broth and bring to a gentle simmer,
- Remove everything from the heat and keep aside, covered for about 10 minutes.
- In the pan with the saffron broth, add 5 1/2 C. of the broth and bring to a gentle simmer and keep on low heat.
- In the same paella pans, divide the artichokes and beans and cook for about 5-6 minutes.
- Transfer the vegetables to a plate.
- Discard the fat from the pans leaving about 1 tbsp in each pan.
- Divide the onion and garlic and sauté till tender.
- Stir in the paprika and pepper flakes and sauté for about 30-60 seconds.
- Divide the tomatoes and cook for about 5-7 minutes.
- Divide the rice, hot saffron broth, chorizo, vegetable mixture and chicken and bring to a boil.
- Reduce the heat to low and simmer, covered for about 5-6 minutes.
- Place the red pepper slices on top of each pan evenly.
- Insert the shrimp in both pans in the rice mixture evenly and simmer for about 10 minutes.
- With foil, cover the pans tightly and simmer or about 2 minutes.
- Increase the heat to medium-high and cook till the bottom layer becomes golden brown.
- Sprinkle the peas evenly and remove everything from the heat and keep aside, covered for about 10 minutes before serving.
- Meanwhile in a pan, add the remaining broth and bring to a boil.

- Add the mussels and simmer, covered for about 3-4 minutes.
- Serve the paella hot with a topping of the mussels and lemon wedges.

Amount per serving: 6

Timing Information:

| Preparation | 30 mins |
| Total Time | 2 hrs |

Nutritional Information:

Calories	952.7
Cholesterol	117.6mg
Sodium	1594.0mg
Carbohydrates	108.2g
Protein	46.3g

* Percent Daily Values are based on a 2,000 calorie diet.

Innovative Paella

Ingredients

- 1/4 C. olive oil
- 16 oz. scallops
- 1 large onion, chopped
- 2 garlic cloves, minced
- 1 1/2 C. rice
- 3 1/4 C. fish stock
- 1/4 tsp saffron
- salt and pepper

- 1 red bell pepper, roasted and cut in strips
- 18 mild green canned chilies
- 1 (14 oz.) can artichoke hearts, drained and sprinkled with lemon juice
- lemon wedge

Directions

- In a paella pan, heat half of the oil on medium-high heat and sauté the scallops for about 3 minutes.
- Transfer the scallops in a bowl and remove the pan liquid.
- In the same pan, heat the remaining oil on medium heat and sauté the onion and garlic for about 5 minutes.
- Stir in the rice and stir fry for about 5 minutes.
- Stir in the saffron, salt, black pepper and broth and simmer for about 10 minutes.
- Stir in the scallops and artichoke and simmer for about 5 minutes.
- Serve hot with a garnishing of lemon wedges and extra roasted bell pepper strips.

Amount per serving: 6

Timing Information:

Preparation	20 mins
Total Time	50 mins

Nutritional Information:

Calories	393.2
Cholesterol	26.1mg
Sodium	539.4mg
Carbohydrates	51.9g
Protein	21.5g

* Percent Daily Values are based on a 2,000 calorie diet.

Paella for Parties

Ingredients

- 2 C. chicken broth
- 3/4 C. dry white wine
- 1/2 tsp saffron thread
- 3 tbsp olive oil
- 6 oz. thin spaghetti, broken into 2-inch lengths
- 6 large shrimp, shelled
- 6 large sea scallops
- 6 clams, scrubbed
- 4 oz. frozen artichoke hearts, thawed
- 1 tsp chives

Directions

- Set your oven to 400 degrees F before doing anything else and arrange a rack in the middle of the oven.
- In a pan, heat the broth and wine and stir in the saffron.
- Keep the pan on low heat.
- In an ovenproof skillet, heat the oil on medium-high heat and stir fry the pasta for about 2 minutes.
- Add the hot broth and simmer for about 5 minutes.

- Insert the seafood into the pasta mixture and cook the mix in the oven for about 20 minutes.
- Serve hot with a garnishing of chives.

Amount per serving: 2

Timing Information:

Preparation	20 mins
Total Time	50 mins

Nutritional Information:

Calories	400.9
Cholesterol	61.8mg
Sodium	928.6mg
Carbohydrates	9.9g
Protein	22.9g

* Percent Daily Values are based on a 2,000 calorie diet.

Paella for Food Lovers

Ingredients

- 1 lb Italian sausage
- 2 tbsp olive oil
- 1 C. sliced onion
- 1 C. sliced green bell pepper
- 1 C. sliced red bell pepper
- 8 chicken thighs (bone-in)
- 1/2 C. dry white wine
- 3 cloves minced garlic
- 4 1/2 C. good-quality chicken broth
- 1/2 tsp saffron strand
- 1 tsp paprika
- 1/4 tsp ground coriander
- 1 bay leaf
- 1/2 tsp thyme
- 1/2 tsp oregano
- salt and pepper
- 2 C. converted rice
- 16 -24 raw shrimp, in the shell
- 3 medium tomatoes, peeled, seeded, juiced, and roughly chopped
- 2 C. diced fresh green beans, blanched 5 minutes
- 1 C. chickpeas, canned
- 1/2 C. black olives, pitted
- 2 lemons, quartered
- parsley sprig

Directions

- With a fork, pierce the sausage and place them in a paella pan with the water.
- Cover and simmer for about 5 minutes.
- Drain well and cut the sausage into 1/2-inch pieces.

- In a paella pan, heat the oil and stir fry the sausage, bell peppers and onion till golden brown.
- Simmer, covered till the vegetables become tender.
- Transfer the sausage mixture into a bowl, leaving the fats in the pan.
- In the same pan, cook the chicken till browned.
- Add the sausage mixture and the remaining ingredients and stir to combine.
- Simmer, covered for about 15 minutes.
- Stir in the rice and boil for about 5-6 minutes.
- Insert the shrimp in the rice mixture, followed by the tomatoes, beans, chickpeas and olives.
- Reduce the heat and simmer, covered for about 8-10 minutes.
- Remove everything from the heat and keep aside, covered for about 5 minutes before serving.
- Serve hot with a garnishing of lemon wedges and parsley.

Amount per serving: 8

Timing Information:

Preparation	35 mins
Total Time	1 hr 20 mins

Nutritional Information:

Calories	640.9
Cholesterol	147.1mg
Sodium	1389.3mg
Carbohydrates	23.9g
Protein	39.9g

* Percent Daily Values are based on a 2,000 calorie diet.

ITALIAN PAELLA

Ingredients

- 2 Italian sausages, removed from casing
- 1/2 red bell pepper, 1/2-inch strips
- 1/2 green bell pepper, 1/2-inch strips
- 1 small onion, 1/2-inch wedges
- 1/2 tbsp olive oil
- 3/4 C. arborio rice
- 1/2 C. dry white wine
- 1 C. tomatoes, canned, drained
- 1 1/2 C. water

Directions

- Set your oven to 400 degrees F before doing anything else.
- In an ovenproof skillet, heat the oil and stir fry the sausage, onion and bell peppers for about 5 minutes.
- Stir in the rice and stir fry for about 1 minute.
- Stir in the remaining ingredients and bring to a boil.
- Now, cook in the oven for about 25 minutes.
- Season with the salt and black pepper and serve.

Amount per serving: 2

Timing Information:

Preparation	10 mins
Total Time	45 mins

Nutritional Information:

Calories	677.2
Cholesterol	47.3mg
Sodium	1016.1mg
Carbohydrates	74.6g
Protein	22.4g

* Percent Daily Values are based on a 2,000 calorie diet.

Paleo Paella

Ingredients

- 10 oz. chorizo sausage
- 2 boneless skinless chicken breasts, cut into bite-size pieces
- 1 tsp paprika
- 1 tsp cumin
- 1/2 tsp salt
- 1/2 tsp pepper
- 1 medium onion, sliced
- 1 red pepper, sliced
- 1 large tomatoes, sliced
- 3 garlic cloves, minced fine
- 1 pinch saffron
- 1 C. chicken broth
- 1/2 head cauliflower, grated with box grater (to resemble rice)

Directions

- In a large pan, cook the chorizo till browned.
- Transfer the chorizo to a plate, leaving the fat in the pan.
- In the same pan, cook the chicken with the cumin, paprika, salt and black pepper and cook till done completely.
- Stir in the pepper and onion and cook till tender.

- Stir in the tomatoes, garlic, salt and black pepper and cook, stirring occasionally till a thick mixture forms.
- Add the saffron and broth and cook, stirring continuously till all the liquid is absorbed.
- Stir in the remaining ingredients and cook the paella until everything is fully done.
- Place the dish in the oven for 10 mins at 350 degrees then let the dish set in the oven for 10 more mins.

Amount per serving: 4

Timing Information:

| Preparation | 15 mins |
| Total Time | 45 mins |

Nutritional Information:

Calories	454.6
Cholesterol	100.2mg
Sodium	1451.0mg
Carbohydrates	12.8g
Protein	33.6g

* Percent Daily Values are based on a 2,000 calorie diet.

Paella in Barcelona Style

Ingredients

- 4 C. water
- 1/2 C. dry white wine
- 2 tbsp black tea
- 1 tbsp oil
- 1 C. snow peas
- 1 C. water chestnut
- 1 red chili
- 1 onion (finely chopped)
- 2 C. rice
- 1 C. dried mango
- 1 kg chicken drumstick

Directions

- In a large paella pan, heat the oil and stir fry the chicken till golden brown.
- Stir in the mangos, onion and chili and cook, stirring occasionally for a few minutes.
- Stir in the rice, tea and 2 C. of the water and cook, stirring occasionally till most of the liquid is absorbed.
- Add the remaining 2 C. of the water and cook, stirring occasionally till all the liquid is absorbed.

- Add the wine and cook till all the liquid is absorbed.
- Stir in the peas and water chestnut and cook till the veggies are heated completely.

Amount per serving: 3

Timing Information:

Preparation	5 mins
Total Time	1 hr 5 mins

Nutritional Information:

Calories	2255.4
Cholesterol	655.0mg
Sodium	662.9mg
Carbohydrates	119.9g
Protein	166.4g

* Percent Daily Values are based on a 2,000 calorie diet.

DENVER STYLE PAELLA

Ingredients

- 1 tbsp olive oil
- 1/2 C. onion, chopped
- 6 oz. chicken sausage, cooked and thinly sliced
- 2 (3 1/2 oz.) packages brown rice (boil-in-bag)
- salt
- 1/2 tsp smoked paprika
- 1/4 tsp black pepper
- 1 (15 oz.) can chicken broth
- 1 (14 1/2 oz.) can diced tomatoes, undrained
- 2 tsp garlic, minced
- 1 1/2 C. edamame, frozen. shelled
- 1/4 tsp saffron thread
- 1/2 lb frozen shrimp, thawed

Directions

- In a large pan, heat the oil on medium-high heat and sauté the sausage and onion till the onions become tender.
- Stir in the rice, paprika, salt and black pepper and sauté for about 30 seconds.
- Add the tomatoes, garlic and broth and bring to a boil.
- Reduce the heat to medium and simmer, covered for about 10 minutes.

- Stir in the remaining ingredients and simmer for about 4 minutes.

Amount per serving: 4

Timing Information:

Preparation	10 mins
Total Time	40 mins

Nutritional Information:

Calories	559.0
Cholesterol	161.5mg
Sodium	1166.4mg
Carbohydrates	62.0g
Protein	37.4g

* Percent Daily Values are based on a 2,000 calorie diet.

Fiesta Paella

Ingredients

- 1/4 C. oil
- 1/4 kg pork
- 3 garlic cloves
- 1/2 chopped onion
- 1 tbsp tomato puree
- 1/2 kg rice
- 1/2 kg shrimp, shelled
- 1/2 chicken
- 100 g chorizo sausage
- 3 green peppers, sliced
- 1 C. peas
- 1 bay leaf
- salt and pepper
- 1 liter water
- 2 links chopped pork sausage
- 1/2 C. squid, chopped
- 1/2 C. crawfish, chopped
- 3 artichoke hearts
- 1/4 kg cockles

Directions

- In a pan of water, boil the cockles till the shells are opened and reserve the cooking water.
- In a large skillet, heat the oil and stir fry all the ingredients except the rice and cockles.
- Add the rice and stir fry till all the liquid is absorbed.
- Add enough reserved cooking water and bring to a boil.
- Simmer till the mixture becomes thick.

- Stir in the cockles and place the pan over a hot plate and cook till the rice is done.
- Remove everything from the heat and keep aside, covered for about 20 minutes before serving.

Amount per serving: 4

Timing Information:

Preparation	30 mins
Total Time	30 mins

Nutritional Information:

Calories	1337.3
Cholesterol	415.8mg
Sodium	1105.0mg
Carbohydrates	122.6g
Protein	88.6g

* Percent Daily Values are based on a 2,000 calorie diet.

Nutritious Paella

Ingredients

- 1/4 C. olive oil
- 5 minced garlic cloves
- 1 large yellow onion, chopped
- 4 C. vegetable broth
- 2 C. rice (uncooked)
- 4 medium tomatoes, skinned, seeded and chopped
- 1 small red bell pepper, seeded and cut into thin strips
- 1 small green bell pepper, seeded and cut into thin strips
- 1 small yellow bell pepper, seeded and cut into thin strips
- 1 C. green peas
- 2 C. artichoke hearts, tough outer leaves removed and quartered
- 1 lemon
- lemon wedge, to garnish

Directions

- In a pan, heat the broth.
- In a large paella pan, heat the oil and sauté the onion and garlic till tender.
- Add the rice and stir fry for about 3 minutes.
- Stir in the tomatoes and bell pepper and stir fry for about 3 minutes.
- Add the hot broth and simmer on medium heat for about 20 minutes.

- Stir in the peas, artichoke and lemon juice and remove everything from the heat.
- Serve hot with a garnishing of lemon wedges.

Amount per serving: 6

Timing Information:

Preparation	30 mins
Total Time	1 hr

Nutritional Information:

Calories	406.0
Cholesterol	0.0mg
Sodium	194.3mg
Carbohydrates	72.7g
Protein	9.3g

* Percent Daily Values are based on a 2,000 calorie diet.

Hearty Paella

Ingredients

- 2 C. water
- 1/2 lb smoked sausage, halved lengthwise and sliced 1/4-inch thick
- 1 (14 1/2 oz.) cans diced tomatoes, undrained
- 1/2 C. chopped onion
- 1 tsp dried parsley flakes
- 1 (7 oz.) packages Yellow Rice
- 1 lb large shrimp, peeled and deveined
- 1 C. frozen peas

Directions

- In a large skillet, mix together the sausage, onion, tomato, parsley and water and bring to a boil.
- Stir in the rice mix and reduce the heat to low.
- Simmer, covered for about 15 minutes.
- Stir in the peas and shrimp and simmer, covered for about 10-15 minutes, stirring occasionally.
- Remove everything from the heat and keep aside, covered for about 5 minutes before serving.

Amount per serving: 8

Timing Information:

Preparation	10 mins
Total Time	40 mins

Nutritional Information:

Calories	154.0
Cholesterol	88.9mg
Sodium	580.0mg
Carbohydrates	5.8g
Protein	12.6g

* Percent Daily Values are based on a 2,000 calorie diet.

Paella in Vegan Style

Ingredients

- 1 pinch saffron thread
- 2 C. vegetable broth
- 1/2 C. water
- 4 vegetarian sausages, cut into 1-inch pieces
- 1 tbsp olive oil, for drizzling
- 1 large onion, chopped
- salt and pepper
- 1/4 C. chopped pimiento
- 1 C. frozen peas
- 1/3 C. dry sherry
- 3 tbsp vegan margarine
- 1/2 C. orzo pasta
- 1 C. brown rice
- 1/2 C. flat leaf parsley, chopped

Directions

- In a pan, mix together 2 C. of the broth, 1/2 C. of the water and saffron on medium heat and bring to a boil.
- Reduce the heat to low and keep covered for a few minutes.
- In a skillet, heat a little oil on medium-high heat and cook the sausage for about 2-3 minutes.
- Transfer the sausage into a bowl.
- In the same skillet, heat a little oil more and sauté the onion, salt and black pepper for about 3 minutes.
- Stir in the peas, pimentos and sherry and cook, stirring for about 1-2 minutes and transfer onto a plate.

- In the same skillet, melt 2 tbsp of the margarine on medium heat and cook the pasta for about 3-4 minutes.
- Add the broth mixture and rice and bring to a boil.
- Reduce the heat to low and simmer, covered for about 18 minutes.
- Meanwhile set your oven to 375 degrees F and grease a casserole dish with the remaining melted margarine.
- Transfer the rice mixture into the prepared casserole dish evenly and top with the onion mixture and sausage.
- Cover the casserole dish loosely and cook in the oven for about 20 minutes.
- Uncover and cook in the oven for about 10 minutes more.
- Serve hot with a garnishing of parsley.

Amount per serving: 6

Timing Information:

Preparation	20 mins
Total Time	55 mins

Nutritional Information:

Calories	269.6
Cholesterol	0.0mg
Sodium	260.0mg
Carbohydrates	42.1g
Protein	9.0g

* Percent Daily Values are based on a 2,000 calorie diet.

FAMILY FRIENDLY PAELLA

Ingredients

- 3 C. water
- 1/2 C. white wine
- 1 1/2 lb. ripe tomatoes, cored and cut into thick wedges
- salt & freshly ground black pepper
- 1/4 C. extra virgin olive oil
- 1 medium onion, minced
- 1 tbsp minced garlic
- 1 tbsp tomato paste
- 1 pinch saffron thread
- 1 -2 tsp paprika
- 2 C. short-grain rice
- minced parsley, and
- basil (to garnish)

Directions

- Set your oven to 450 degrees F before doing anything else.
- In a pan, warm the water.
- In a bowl, add the tomatoes, 1 tbsp of the oil salt and black pepper and toss to coat well.

- In a 12-inch ovenproof skillet, heat the remaining oil on medium-high heat and sauté the bell pepper, onion, garlic, salt and black pepper for about 3-5 minutes.
- Stir in the tomato paste, saffron and paprika and sauté for about 1 minute.
- Add the rice and stir fry for about 1-2 minutes.
- Add the wine and cook till all the liquid is absorbed then stir in the hot water.
- Place the tomato mixture over the rice mixture and cook in the oven for about 15 minutes.
- If rice is dry and not done completely, then add the required amount of broth and cook everything in the oven for about 5-10 mins more.
- Turn off the oven but keep the pan inside for about 5-15 minutes before serving.
- Serve with a topping of the basil and parsley.

Amount per serving: 4

Timing Information:

Preparation	10 mins
Total Time	40 mins

Nutritional Information:

Calories	551.8
Cholesterol	0.0mg
Sodium	47.8mg
Carbohydrates	91.1g
Protein	8.6g

* Percent Daily Values are based on a 2,000 calorie diet.

FLAVOR-PACKED PAELLA

Ingredients

- 3 lb. chicken, chopped into medium chunks
- 1 tbsp olive oil
- 8 oz. cooked sausage, sliced
- 1 onion, sliced
- 3 tsp garlic, minced
- 2 tsp dried thyme
- 1 1/4 tsp pepper
- 1 tsp paprika
- 1/8 tsp saffron
- 1/2 tsp turmeric
- 14 1/2 oz. chicken broth
- 1/2 C. water
- 2 yellow peppers, diced
- 1 C. green peas
- 3 C. cooked rice

Directions

- In a large pan, heat the oil and stir fry the chicken till golden brown.
- Drain the excess fat and transfer the chicken into the slow cooker with sausage, onion, garlic, saffron, thyme and spices.
- Pour the water and broth and set the slow cooker on low settings.
- Cover and cook for about 8 hours.
- Uncover the slow cooker and immediately, stir in the peas, tomatoes and peppers.
- Serve the chicken mixture over the rice.

Amount per serving: 4

Timing Information:

Preparation	15 mins
Total Time	5 hrs 15 mins

Nutritional Information:

Calories	1227.5
Cholesterol	302.7mg
Sodium	1008.2mg
Carbohydrates	56.0g
Protein	83.4g

* Percent Daily Values are based on a 2,000 calorie diet.

VERSATILE PAELLA

Ingredients

- 1 tbsp vegetable oil
- 1 lb chicken sausage, sliced diagonally
- 1 small onion, finely chopped
- 2 garlic cloves, finely chopped
- 1 red bell pepper, unseeded, cut into strips
- 4 C. low chicken broth
- 1 (14 oz.) cans diced tomatoes
- 1 (16 oz.) packages Spanish rice mix
- 4 oz. cooked ham, chopped
- 1 C. frozen peas
- salt

Directions

- In a large skillet, heat 1 tbsp of the oil on medium-high heat and cook the sausage for about 5 minutes.
- Transfer the sausage into a slow cooker.
- In the same skillet, sauté the onion, bell pepper and garlic for about 3-5 minutes and transfer into the slow cooker.
- In the same skillet, add 1 cup of the broth on high heat and bring to a boil, stirring continuously and pour into a slow cooker.

- Add the remaining ingredients except the peas and set the slow cooker on low.
- Cover and cook for about 4 hours.
- Uncover the slow cooker and stir in the peas and cook, covered for about 15 minutes more.

Amount per serving: 6

Timing Information:

Preparation	20 mins
Total Time	24 mins

Nutritional Information:

Calories	307.8
Cholesterol	108.5mg
Sodium	1013.0mg
Carbohydrates	18.2g
Protein	20.7g

* Percent Daily Values are based on a 2,000 calorie diet.

COMFORT BROWN RICE PAELLA

Ingredients

- 1 lb extra-large shrimp, peeled and deveined
- salt & freshly ground black pepper
- olive oil
- 8 -9 medium garlic cloves
- 1 lb chicken thigh
- 1 red bell pepper, seeded and cut pole to pole into 1/2-inch-wide strips
- 8 oz. spanish chorizo, sliced 1/2 inch thick on the bias
- 1 medium onion, chopped fine
- 1 (14 1/2 oz.) cans diced tomatoes, drained, minced, and drained again
- 2 C. long grain brown rice
- 3 C. low chicken broth
- 1/3 C. dry white wine
- 1/2 tsp saffron thread, crumbled
- 1 bay leaf
- 1 dozen mussels, scrubbed and debearded
- 1/2 C. frozen green pea, thawed
- 2 tsp fresh parsley leaves
- 1 lemon, cut into wedges, for serving

Directions

- Set your oven to 350 degrees F before doing anything else and arrange the oven rack to lower-middle position.

- In s bowl, add the shrimp, 1 tsp of the garlic, 1 tbsp of the oil, salt and black pepper and toss to coat well.
- Refrigerate, covered till serving.
- In another bowl, add the chicken and season with the salt and black pepper.
- In a large Dutch oven, heat 2 tsp of the oil on medium-high heat and sauté the peppers for about 3-4 minutes.
- Transfer the peppers into a plate.
- In the same pan, heat 1 tsp of the oil and cook the chicken for about 3 minutes.
- Transfer the chicken into another plate.
- Reduce the heat to medium and cook the chorizo for about 4-5 minutes.
- Transfer the chorizo in the plate with the chicken.
- In the same Dutch oven, heat 2 tbsp of the oil on medium heat and sauté the onion for about 3 minutes.
- Add the remaining garlic and sauté for about 1 minute.
- Add the tomatoes and cook for about 3 minutes.
- Add the rice and stir fry for about 1-2 minutes.
- Add the wine, broth, saffron, bay leaf and salt and bring to a boil on medium-high heat.
- Cover and cook in the oven for about 30 minutes.
- Stir in the chicken and chorizo, cover and cook in the oven for about 15 minutes.
- Insert the mussels in rice mixture, hinged side down and place the shrimp over rice.
- Top with the peppers, cover and cook in the oven for about 12 minutes.
- Remove from the oven and keep aside, covered for about 5 minutes before serving.

- Serve hot with a garnishing of parsley and lemon wedges.

Amount per serving: 6

Timing Information:

Preparation	20 mins
Total Time	1 hr 8 mins

Nutritional Information:

Calories	747.5
Cholesterol	220.7mg
Sodium	933.3mg
Carbohydrates	64.3g
Protein	50.6g

* Percent Daily Values are based on a 2,000 calorie diet.

Traditional Restaurant Style Paella

Ingredients

- 1/4 C. olive oil
- 1/2 C. onion, chopped
- 1 tsp garlic, finely chopped
- 1 medium-size sweet red peppers or 1 green pepper, seeded, deribbed and cut into strips
- 8 pieces asparagus
- 1 tomatoes, chopped
- 1/2 C. fresh peas
- 1/2 tsp saffron, ground
- 8 medium-size mushrooms, sliced
- salt & pepper
- 2 artichokes, cut in quarters
- 6 C. boiling water
- 3 C. medium grain rice

Directions

- Set your oven to 400 degrees F before doing anything else.
- In a large deep ovenproof skillet, heat the oil on medium heat and stir fry the vegetables for about 1 minute.
- Stir in the rice, salt, black pepper and water and bring to a boil.

- Stir in the saffron and arrange the skillet on the floor of the oven.
- Cook for about 20 minutes.
- Remove from the oven and keep aside, covered for about 5 minutes before serving.

Amount per serving: 4

Timing Information:

| Preparation | 10 mins |
| Total Time | 60 mins |

Nutritional Information:

Calories	747.9
Cholesterol	0.0mg
Sodium	91.4mg
Carbohydrates	136.8g
Protein	17.5g

* Percent Daily Values are based on a 2,000 calorie diet.

SUPER QUICK PAELLA

Ingredients

- 2 tbsp oil
- 1/2 lb small scallops
- 2 garlic cloves, crushed
- 1 1/3 C. Minute Rice
- 1 tbsp cornstarch
- 1 1/4 C. chicken broth
- 1 (14 1/2 oz.) cans diced tomatoes
- 1/2 C. pepperoni, thinly sliced
- 1/2 C. frozen green pea
- 1/4 tsp Tabasco sauce

Directions

- In a pan, heat the oil and stir fry the scallops and garlic for about 2 minutes.
- Stir in the cornstarch and cook, stirring for about 1 minute.
- Stir in the remaining ingredients except the rice and bring to boil.
- Stir in the rice and immediately cover the pan and remove from the heat.
- Remove everything from the heat and keep aside, covered for about 5 minutes before serving.

Amount per serving: 4

Timing Information:

Preparation	2 mins
Total Time	10 mins

Nutritional Information:

Calories	303.1
Cholesterol	86.4mg
Sodium	571.2mg
Carbohydrates	38.1g
Protein	17.3g

* Percent Daily Values are based on a 2,000 calorie diet.

PAELLA FOR SPRINGTIME

Ingredients

- 5 C. chicken broth
- 1/4 tsp saffron thread
- 1 1/2 lb. loin lamb, trimmed of any surface fat and cut into 1-inch pieces
- 1/2 tsp salt
- 1/2 tsp fresh ground black pepper
- 3 tbsp olive oil
- 6 oz. thick-cut pancetta, diced
- 1 large leek, white and pale green parts, sliced in half lengthwise, then thinly sliced
- 8 baby artichokes, halved, dark outer leaves removed, and stems trimmed
- 1 C. dry light white wine
- 2 tbsp chopped rosemary
- 2 1/2 C. arborio rice
- 1 1/2 C. shelled fresh peas

Directions

- Set your oven to 375 degrees F before doing anything else and arrange the oven rack in the center position.
- In a pan, mix together the broth and saffron on low heat and heat till just warmed.
- Cover and keep aside.
- Season the lamb with the salt and black pepper.
- In a paella pan, heat the oil on medium heat and cook the lamb for about 6 minutes.

- Transfer the lamb into a bowl.
- In the same pan, stir fry the pancetta for about 4 minutes.
- Stir in the leek and cook for about 3 minutes.
- Stir in the artichoke and cook for about 1 minute.
- Stir in the rosemary and wine and cook, stirring once for about 5 minutes.
- Stir in the rice and cook for about 1 minute.
- Add the warm broth and bring to a boil.
- Reduce the heat and simmer, stirring occasionally for about 10 minutes.
- Insert the lamb pieces into the rice mixture and top everything with the peas evenly.
- Cook the dish in the oven for about 15 minutes.
- Remove everything from the oven and keep aside, covered for about 10 minutes before serving.

Amount per serving: 6

Timing Information:

Preparation	1 hr
Total Time	1 hr 55 mins

Nutritional Information:

Calories	873.9
Cholesterol	83.9mg
Sodium	1021.5mg
Carbohydrates	88.7g
Protein	34.4g

* Percent Daily Values are based on a 2,000 calorie diet.

Paella in Hawaiian Style

Ingredients

- 12 large shrimp, peeled and deveined
- achiote paste, as required
- 1 tbsp olive oil
- 4 tbsp onions, small dice
- 1/2 C. chicken stock
- 1 lb yellow tomatoes, chopped
- 1 tsp yellow bell pepper, chopped
- 24 manila clams, washed
- 8 large basil leaves, torn
- cilantro leaf, torn
- salt

Directions

- In a bowl, mix together the shrimp and achiote paste and refrigerate to marinate for about 20 minutes.
- In a Dutch oven, heat the oil and sauté the onion till tender.
- Add the broth and bring to a boil and stir in the bell pepper, tomatoes and clams.
- Cook, covered for about 7 minutes.
- Stir in the shrimp and cook, covered till done completely.

- Serve with a garnishing of cilantro and basil.

Amount per serving: 2

Timing Information:

Preparation	20 mins
Total Time	40 mins

Nutritional Information:

Calories	301.2
Cholesterol	99.3mg
Sodium	1388.8mg
Carbohydrates	17.6g
Protein	34.7g

* Percent Daily Values are based on a 2,000 calorie diet.

Yummy Paella Bites

Ingredients

- 2 1/2 C. short grain rice
- 1 large onion, medium chopped
- 1 bay leaf
- 2 tsp crushed garlic
- 1 chicken bouillon cube
- 1 1/2 tsp saffron, crushed
- 1 tbsp olive oil
- 5 C. chicken stock, heated
- 6 oz. salami
- 6 oz. smoked ham
- seasoned flour
- Egg wash
- 2 eggs, beaten with
- 1 little milk
- seasoned dry bread crumb
- oil, to fry
- parsley, to serve

Directions

- In a large pan, mix together the rice, bouillon cube, garlic, bay leaf, saffron and olive oil.
- Add the broth and bring to a boil and simmer for about 17 minutes.
- Remove everything from the heat and discard the bay leaf.
- Keep aside to cool completely.
- In a food processor, add the meats and pulse till chopped finely.
- Add the meat mixture in the cooled rice mixture and mix well.
- Make medium sized balls from the mixture.
- In a shallow dish, place the seasoned flour.

- In a second shallow dish, place the egg wash.
- In a third shallow dish, place the breadcrumbs.
- Coat the rice balls in the flour and then dip in the egg wash.
- Now, roll the balls into breadcrumbs.
- Arrange the balls into a baking dish and refrigerate, covered overnight.
- In a large skillet, heat the oil to 365 degrees F and deep fry the balls till golden brown.
- Serve with a garnishing of parsley.

Amount per serving: 1

Timing Information:

Preparation	25 mins
Total Time	55 mins

Nutritional Information:

Calories	108.6
Cholesterol	32.3mg
Sodium	385.2mg
Carbohydrates	9.9g
Protein	5.8g

* Percent Daily Values are based on a 2,000 calorie diet.

Delicious Paella

Ingredients

- 1/2 lemon
- 1 1/4 oz. frozen peas
- 2 chicken thighs
- 1 fluid oz. chicken stock
- 1 -2 clove garlic, crushed
- 1 fluid oz. olive oil
- pepper
- 4 1/2 oz. rice
- 1 saffron thread
- 1 pinch dried thyme
- 1 pinch dried rosemary
- 1 onion, chopped
- 2 -3 oz. seafood
- salt

Directions

- For the seafood use a combo of the prawns, quid, clams and mussels.
- In a large pan, heat the oil and stir fry the chicken, onion and garlic till golden brown.
- Stir in the rice and cook, stirring continuously for about 1 minute.

- Add the crushed saffron, herbs and broth and bring to a boil and simmer for about 15 minutes.
- Stir in the seafood and cook till all the liquid is absorbed.
- Stir in the peas, salt and black pepper.
- Cover the pan and remove everything from the heat and keep aside for about 10 minutes.
- Serve hot with a garnishing of lemon wedges and warm brown bread.

Amount per serving: 2

Timing Information:

Preparation	25 mins
Total Time	51 mins

Nutritional Information:

Calories	598.3
Cholesterol	79.4mg
Sodium	97.0mg
Carbohydrates	62.8g
Protein	22.7g

* Percent Daily Values are based on a 2,000 calorie diet.

Vegetarian Friendly Paella

Ingredients

- 1/2 tsp saffron thread
- 2 tbsp hot water
- 3 tbsp olive oil
- 1 large onion, chopped
- 1 zucchini, coarsely chopped
- 2 garlic cloves, crushed
- 1/4 tsp cayenne pepper
- 8 oz. tomatoes, peeled, cut into wedges
- 15 oz. canned chick-peas, drained
- 15 oz. canned artichoke hearts, drained, coarsely sliced
- 1 1/2 C. medium grain rice
- 5 1/2 C. vegetable stock, simmering
- 5 1/2 oz. green beans, blanched
- salt and pepper
- 1 lemon, cut into wedges, for serving

Directions

- In a small bowl, add the water and saffron threads and keep aside for a few minutes.
- In a skillet, heat the oil and sauté the zucchini and onion for about 2-3 minutes.
- Stir in the saffron mixture, garlic and cayenne pepper and sauté for about 1 minute.
- Stir in the chickpeas, tomato and artichokes and stir fry for about 2 minutes.
- Stir in the rice and cook, stirring continuously for about 1 minute.

- Add most of the broth and bring to a boil and simmer for about 10 minutes, shaking the pan once or twice.
- Add the green beans, salt and black pepper and shake the pan to combine.
- Simmer for about 10-15 minutes. (Add more broth if required)
- Remove everything from the heat and immediately cover the pan with foil paper and keep aside for about 5 minutes.
- Serve hot with a drizzling of the lemon juice.

Amount per serving: 1

Timing Information:

Preparation	20 mins
Total Time	55 mins

Nutritional Information:

Calories	601.1
Cholesterol	0.0mg
Sodium	426.1mg
Carbohydrates	109.1g
Protein	16.2g

* Percent Daily Values are based on a 2,000 calorie diet.

PICNIC PAELLA SALAD

Ingredients

- 2 (5 oz.) packages saffron yellow rice
- 1/4 C. balsamic vinegar
- 1/4 C. lemon juice
- 1 tbsp olive oil
- 1 tsp dried basil leaves
- 1/8 tsp pepper
- 1 dash cayenne pepper
- 1 lb medium shrimp, cooked and peeled
- 1 (14 oz.) can artichoke hearts, drained
- 3/4 C. green bell pepper, chopped
- 1 C. frozen green pea, thawed
- 1 C. tomatoes, chopped
- 1 (2 oz.) jar diced pimentos, drained
- 1/2 C. red onion, chopped
- 2 oz. prosciutto, chopped

Directions

- Cook the rice according to package's directions, omitting the salt and oil.
- In a bowl, add the oil, lemon juice, vinegar, basil, cayenne pepper and black pepper and mix well.
- In another large bowl, mix together the cooked rice and the remaining ingredients.
- Add the dressing and toss to coat well.
- Refrigerate, covered for about 2 hours before serving.

Amount per serving: 6

Timing Information:

Preparation	20 mins
Total Time	50 mins

Nutritional Information:

Calories	171.8
Cholesterol	95.5mg
Sodium	523.5mg
Carbohydrates	21.0g
Protein	15.3g

* Percent Daily Values are based on a 2,000 calorie diet.

THANKS FOR READING! JOIN THE CLUB AND KEEP ON COOKING WITH 6 MORE COOKBOOKS....

http://bit.ly/1TdrStv

 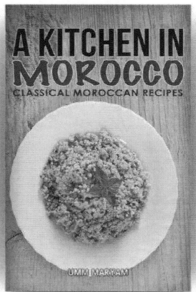 

To grab the box sets simply follow the link mentioned above, or tap one of book covers.

This will take you to a page where you can simply enter your email address and a PDF version of the box sets will be emailed to you.

Hope you are ready for some serious cooking!

http://bit.ly/1TdrStv

COME ON...
LET'S BE FRIENDS :)

We adore our readers and love connecting with them socially.

Like BookSumo on Facebook and let's get social!

Facebook

And also check out the BookSumo Cooking Blog.

Food Lover Blog

Made in the USA
Lexington, KY
31 August 2017